Providence

True Stories of God's

Direction and Protection

Ann Haerr

ESTATE PUBLISHING

LA QUINTA

Providence

First Printing, 2015

Estate Publishing

La Quinta

Printed in the United States of America

Cover photo Carlos Koblischek

Guest Editor Kevin Haerr

Dedication

This book is dedicated to women of all ages.

I encourage you to spend more time by yourself and alone in prayer so you can find out who you truly are and learn to love yourself.

Don't waste as much time as I did.

Providence

Providence

True Stories of God's Direction and Protection

Providence

Table of Contents

"Blessed Assurance"

By Frances J Crosby, 1873

Blessed assurance, Jesus is mine!
Oh, what a foretaste of glory divine!
Heir of salvation, purchase of God,
Born of His Spirit, washed in His blood.

This is my story, this is my song,
Praising my Savior all the day long;
This is my story, this is my song,
Praising my Savior all the day long.

Perfect submission, perfect delight,
Visions of rapture now burst on my sight;
Angels, descending, bring from above
Echoes of mercy, whispers of love.

Perfect submission, all is at rest,
I in my Savior am happy and blest,
Watching and waiting, looking above,
Filled with His goodness, lost in His love.

This is my story, this is my song,
Praising my Savior all the day long;
This is my story, this is my song,
Praising my Savior all the day long.

Providence

Acknowledgement

Thank you to my husband, Kevin,
for encouraging me to find my own voice.

Without your love and support, life would not
be nearly as musical or as much fun.

Providence

Introduction

I was a sad and lonely girl most of my life. I never really understood who I was or why I was here. I believed that I was unwanted and unloved. Sadly, I wasted so many years searching for someone to care, and although I thought I had it all together, I really did not have a clue.

I made so many poor choices, tolerated so much and put myself at terrible risk, more than once. It is only by the grace of God that I was not horribly hurt or left for dead, and that I was blessed with life into adulthood and beyond.

I am more than a bit embarrassed to say it, but these short stories are true and just a few from many experiences in my past. Each story was originally written to stand alone, and some are simple and some are more intense. But together, they will give you a glimpse into my journey. It has been a long road, but I have finally understood my purpose and the unending love of God.

I have had many amazing mentors, especially some from during the past ten years. I am very grateful for them, because I have learned so much about becoming my best. I cherish my teachers and will continue studying for the rest of my life.

In reading these stories, I hope you will get a sense of how God has always been right by my side through it all, allowing me to learn and grow, even when I neglected to appreciate His grace. He is so faithful, and has brought me through so much. I am no longer that sad little girl, and I know exactly who I am.

A Rough Start

My parents had prayed for me before I was born. They were Christians and trusted God for His direction, blessings and faithfulness. I was brought into the world and then dedicated to the Lord when I was just weeks old.

My mother had contracted the chicken pox while she was pregnant with me, and had to worry and wonder if I would be born with any birth defects. Medicine had not had a lot of the advances yet which have been made during the past few decades, so it was a very tense time for my parents.

The pregnancy was far enough along to know that I had been fully formed but was still in the process of growing before I would be big enough to come into the world. No one could say for sure if or how I might be affected. So between the doctor doing all he could and a lot of prayers being offered from a lot of people, both my parents waited anxiously for me to be born and hoped for a strong, healthy baby.

I was carried to full term and appeared to be fine when I was born, although I was very small. So small, in fact, that when the doctor delivered me, he held me up and announced, "It's a peanut!" It turned out that I had not received much nourishment during the last month of the pregnancy due to the virus attacking the placenta. But other than size, thankfully, everything else seemed to be normal.

My parents had to leave me at the hospital for quite a while until I got up to a weight of five pounds. So it was a difficult time for them feeling both happiness and sadness simultaneously. They were thankful I was healthy but wanted to take me home. In time, it all worked out, except that the nurses were busy during the day and let me sleep then. When things calmed down in the evening, the nurses kept me up and played with me all night. So it took quite a while to get me on a regular schedule when I finally did go home.

There was not a "Premie" industry yet at that time, so my parents had to buy doll clothes to dress me in. They had prayed for children, and after nine years had been given first my older brother and then me. They knew we were blessed and that God had His hand on us through it all.

Even to this day, I exhibit traits which I believe came about because of those early times of my life. I am definitely a "night owl" and could stay up all night if needed, yet mornings are most difficult for me. So I guess I have those nurses to thank for that. Also, I am always hungry, or at least I can honestly say that food is a definite preoccupation of mine. I often wonder if that is because in my unconscious mind, I remember and wonder if I may go unfed for a while like when I was in the womb. I do not know, but it is curious to think about. I am just so glad that God has given me health, strength, clarity and vision. I am able to look back and am amazed at a life which started badly is still going strong today.

Providence

Child's Play

As children do, my brother and I played together all the time when we were little. We were only seventeen months apart and I adored him. So because he was a boy and he was the older child, we would often play what he wanted, which was usually baseball.

Being very young, neither of us were very good at throwing or catching. But we tried hard and had fun playing with each other. No doubt, he would have rather had some boys his own age to play with, but since there were none available, he had to make do with me.

One day when we were outside playing, I apparently was not meeting his expectations because he got mad at me. So as kids do when they do not know how to vent their frustrations, my loving brother came over and hit me in the head with the baseball bat.

Of course, I screamed and cried and ran into the house to tattle on him. My parents could not believe what he had done and he got reprimanded. Soon he was crying too. My mother checked my "wound" which was probably more emotional than physical, and she soothed my aching head. I think I was only three years old at the time, so I do not remember much of anything other than getting hit and crying a lot.

After maybe an hour or so, when both my brother and I were feeling better, we were back to normal and being friendly again and went back outside to play. We must not have had much else to do because we started playing baseball again. It was not long before my brother got mad at me again, mostly that I had gotten him in trouble, and he handled it by hitting me in the head with the bat AGAIN!

So we went through all the tears and trouble one more time that day, which is just how siblings often do. I know we went on to play baseball a lot more while we were growing up since we were often each other's only playmate until my younger brother came along.

While I suppose my brother could have really injured me at the time and could have caused long-term effects, I really do not think that was his intention (at least I hope not). Thankfully, I must have a really hard head because we both grew up strong and healthy.

Sudden Illness

I had been small when I was born, but I grew normally and was a happy little girl. Thankfully, there did not seem to be any residual effects from the chicken pox my mother had during her pregnancy. But when I was just four years old, my parents noticed that I appeared bloated and pale. I was not complaining of any pain and still had energy. But one day, I ran to get my mother after going to the bathroom. I wanted to show her how "red" it was in the toilet. I did not know it at the time, but that was blood in my urine.

After rushing to the hospital, it was determined that I had a kidney disease, called glomerulonephritis. (It took me years to be able to say that correctly.) That illness occurs when the small hairs inside the kidneys which filter the blood are inflamed and bleeding. The doctors told my parents that it was extremely serious, because if they did not heal properly, the kidneys would not work correctly, which could be potentially fatal.

Doctors did not have the ability then provide dialysis like they do today, and antibiotics were fairly new on the medical scene. But I was given the new, promising wonder drug, penicillin, and similar new derivatives at the time. I was in the hospital for several weeks and only remember being frightened when getting injections every day. I was one sick little girl, and my family kept vigil in both person and in prayer.

God amazingly brought me through it and the day came when I finally was allowed to go home, although I was still confined to bed rest for several more months. My father, who was a medical resident at the hospital then, had to take my blood every week to check my progress. I remember how afraid it made me, and I still have a fear of needles today. But it had to be difficult for my father as well, especially since he had to take blood from my ankles because my arms and veins were so tiny. I am sure I did not make it easy for him, and it must have been very good practice to have a screaming child as a patient.

I did eventually heal and got back to a normal childhood. I loved to play with my brother, sing with my parents and go to school. Thankfully, I was healed completely and have not had any other problems related to that kidney illness. It could have been potentially devastating in many ways and could have given me life-long health problems. But God had another plan for me and I have been blessed with good health since that time.

Providence

Winter in Arkansas

Arkansas is a beautiful state, and very different than California. The seasons there are much more defined, with the winters often being cold and rainy.

One year our family flew back to visit relatives, and I remember how pretty it was there even though I had to wear several layers of clothing. My mother needed to go into town and obviously did not have a car to drive. So she borrowed a vehicle from my grandmother and took me with her to the store.

Of course, my Mom was plenty experienced at driving and had done so for many years prior. But driving in the rain can always be treacherous, especially when you are not familiar with the roads or the area or are driving someone else's car.

It was a fairly rural area outside of Bentonville, and I remember the trees being bare and us passing occasional farmhouses. We were on a straight two lane road with very little traffic, and to the right of us was a ditch paralleling the street.

We knew it was a rainy day and had prepared for that. But what my mother did not know was that it was cold enough to cause the water building up on the roads to begin freezing. All of a sudden, she hit a patch of ice and began losing control of the car.

We started to spin and I saw the car moving closer to the ditch. My mother was trying to recover the car, but it moved off the road and far enough over to where it should have dropped down into the ditch. But when the car finally stopped spinning, we were somehow back over on the road.

Both my mother and I sat there shaking for several minutes before she could compose herself. She made sure I was alright and said a little prayer of thanks, with neither of us knowing exactly how we had survived the spinout. We just looked at each other in amazement because we both knew we should have landed down in that ditch.

There was no explanation for the car moving back over to the road, but we knew God had kept us safe. If we had crashed, we could have been killed or hurt badly and no one would have found us for hours. Needless to say, my Mom drove a lot slower than usual to the store and back after that experience.

Times Have Changed

When I was still a teenager, I had a supervisor at work who easily could have been accused of sexual harassment. At least today he would be, for sure. But times were different then. Plus, I was young and naïve and did not know any better.

This man would call me into his office and close the door. Sometimes he would talk to me about something work related, but most times he would just sit behind his desk and stare and smile at me. It was always very uncomfortable as he sat there grinning from ear to ear and not saying anything. But I thought he was just being funny and I had never been subjected to something like that before. I still do not know what was going on under that desk or if he was just hoping for something more while we were alone together.

Other times he would pat my arms or rub my back before he sat down. I just thought he was very friendly, and that was better than some of the mean supervisors I had before him. I thought he was married so did not think he was wanting anything except a working relationship. Nothing else ever occurred to me, and he never said anything that seemed

13

unusually out of place. But I never knew what to think or what to do. So I would sit there and answer his questions when he talked, and simply smile when he would sit and stare at me.

Maybe he liked making girls uncomfortable. I know I was not the only girl who got called into his office. But this man had worked at the company for a long time, and no one seemed to think he behaved out of the ordinary. I cannot imagine that they did not know he was often unprofessional, especially since I was not the only girl being harassed. But I wonder if anyone ever complained because harassment was not defined like it is today, and we did not even know exactly what to complain about. This man was important and well known in the company after all, so who would believe us?

Fortunately, I got transferred to another department and did not have to work with that supervisor anymore. But it was creepy and I was thankful that the situation never got any worse.

Years later, I know that man is retired now. If I had known what was happening all those years ago, I would have taken steps to make sure someone at least knew what he was doing. I really do not think he ever hurt anyone physically, but I have no way of knowing. It was emotionally disturbing but did teach me a good lesson about professionalism in the workplace.

Providence

Living Scared

As I grew up, my mother helped put my father through medical school and my father had become a doctor. When he graduated and opened his practice, they worked together and my mother assisted him for many years.

I cannot say what caused the deterioration of their relationship, but their marriage became strained and dysfunctional. There had apparently been different issues for years, and my mother put up with a lot of things, including my father's temper and infidelity.

As an adult, I know it takes two to make a marriage. So I know my mother was not perfect either and that a lot goes into making a relationship work. But what I do know for sure is what a difficult life my brothers and I had witnessing abuse, and how unsettled our lives were after my parents divorced.

My mother was not good at handling money, even though she kept working at the time. But she was not at all herself and life became very chaotic, even more so than before my father left us. She was still driving us across town to school, but often sent us with odd lunches because of not having normal groceries in the house. I remember being embarrassed by the sandwiches we ate, although I was happy to at least have something for lunch.

The bills piled up, and all too often phone calls were being ignored, resulting in hateful messages from bill collectors. Laws have changed since then, but at the time, those strangers would come banging on our door, and would often be waiting for us outside.

To further complicate the situation, my poor mother would come home after work exhausted, and the only coping skill she seemed to have was relaxing with a cheap bottle of wine. I do not believe she was an alcoholic, but all too often she would go to sleep on the sofa leaving us kids unattended. My brother and I were two young teenagers who were left to care for a younger sibling, which only caused us additional friction and resentment.

I remember feeling alone and scared so much of the time, and I was so sad that my father was gone. It was hard to believe that he cared for us at all when our lifestyle was so disorderly and in such a downward spiral. I was indignant and angry, but had been taught to forgive. So although I did not feel at fault for the problems, I certainly felt confused and helpless to change the situation at all.

We eventually were forced to move, but things never really did get any better. My mother had emotional and financial problems the rest of her life, and I developed personality issues which I have only recently come to understand.

I finally moved out on my own when I was nineteen, and I began my own life. It has been a series of interesting choices since then, many of which related to how I learned to cope in that early environment.

Once I was able to look back at it all, I learned that there is always more than one side to every story, and that people have different coping skills. Somehow God used those negative experiences to help make me empathetic and stronger.

Providence

Lounge Lizard

I was brought up as a Christian, and my parents and grandparents loved God and taught me about Him. That included many aspects of a faith-based environment, including prayer, church, Sunday school, gospel music and private education through high school. My parents also had a music ministry where they would sing and give their testimonies at different churches. But sadly, my parents had issues and did not stay married.

When I was a teenager, I was a mess. My parents had gone through a horrible divorce after twenty-four years of marriage, and my father was getting ready to remarry. I did not understand what had happened at all, how my father could abandon us and go create a second family, or why he did not seem to love me. So even though I had been raised in a Christian home (however dysfunctional it was), I was sad and lonely and was looking anywhere and everywhere for someone to care for me.

I had been very sheltered and was not familiar with the ways of the world. Of course, I thought I was mature and able to handle anything that came my way. I became pretty rebellious and tried more and more to assert my independence, even when putting myself at obvious risk.

One of the local restaurants was a family favorite, and it had a lounge area with a bar where patrons could have a drink while waiting for their tables. I had been in that area a few times with my mother, and often we would see kids in there with their parents. It was more of a bar atmosphere on the weekends when they would have a band and live music.

A girlfriend and I began spending time there on Friday and Saturday nights, trying to act as adults. Fortunately, the band members got to know us and I even dated one of them. Not to say that was a good situation at all, but at least the guys kept an eye on us and would have noticed if anyone had tried to take advantage of two young, pretty, really dumb girls.

I remember that the management of the restaurant was not happy to see us when we would be there. They knew we were underage, but surprisingly, they did not kick us out. Some older men did try to engage me or ask me out occasionally, and I was way too friendly to strangers. But it was a place for me to be where I felt autonomous, and I walked around like I owned the place. Like most young girls, I really believed the guy I was dating cared for me, even though he was older and we were not even close to being on the same page of life.

But I am thankful for that band at that time, whose members fueled my love of music but were also apparently used by God to keep me safe whether they knew it or not. It was a confusing and vulnerable time in my life and I could have gotten into a lot of trouble.

Providence

Singing at a Concert

During the 1970's, my mother was dating a musician who gave voice lessons. I was learning from this teacher who had some well-known and interesting clients. He offered the lessons at his home, and one of his students was half of a celebrity musical duo. Often I would have a lesson right after this fellow student, so I would enjoy listening to him vocalize as I waited for my appointment time.

At some point that year, this particular musical duo was giving a concert at the Greek Theater in Los Angeles. They asked my vocal coach to put together a few of his people to have a group of singers to sing backup on some of their songs at the concert. I was fortunate to be in that group of singers.

If you have been to the Greek Theater, you know that it is in the Griffith Park area of Los Angeles. To get there, you have to drive way up a hill through a neighborhood of older, beautiful homes, and the street narrows as the road goes higher. You can turn off into parking lots as you pass the theater, but it then becomes a tight, winding mountain road.

I was still a teenager at the time, so my mother had driven me to the concert. She had a big, old Cadillac then which was like a tank. After the concert, we got into the car and my Mom started slowly moving into traffic to go down the hill and then to the freeway. As you can imagine, the traffic was terrible, and pretty much stopped due to the concert just letting out.

I remember my mother starting to drive but then having a look of horror on her face. She was frantically pumping the brakes only to find that they were not working. I do not know what had happened, as they had been working fine on our way to the venue. They may have needed fluid, or they may have overheated or had some other issue. I do not know if my mother ever really found out what had gone wrong.

As she was beginning to panic and yell, I remember her trying to do whatever she could to stop the car. She kept pumping the brakes, she tried putting the car in park, and she may have even turned the key to shut off the motor. It all happened so quickly. But the car was beginning to move faster and faster, and we were picking up speed as we started rolling down that hill. There was traffic, so I do not even know how to explain how there was room for the car to be moving in the lane we were in.

I remember my Mom looking frantically around to see any place where she might turn to get out of traffic. She could move out of our lane slightly as she passed one of the driveways to another parking lot, although there was still traffic coming out of the lots. The car was moving fast as we were quickly approaching stopped traffic up ahead.

Just before we were going to hit the back of a car which was completely stopped, my mother somehow drove over a big dip in the road. Neither of us had seen it at all, but by hitting the dip, the car slowed down just enough so that it did not kill anyone when we slammed into those poor people ahead of us.

There were three or four people in that car, two of whom were in the back seat and got thrown into the front seat. I think it was an older couple and their family, and of course, they were all shocked from the jolt as we were. But thankfully, they had not been completely wiped out as they could have been if our car had not slowed down.

It was so interesting too, how neither my mother nor I were seriously hurt or thrown through the windshield during the crash. I think we both had seat (lap) belts on, but I do not remember for sure. I know we did not have shoulder belts like vehicles have today. It turned out that we both had bruises in the exact same spots, and only on our knees! It was as if there was a big arm holding us both back so that when we crashed, we were held in but moved forward enough so that our knees hit the dashboard hard. I do not remember much else about it, but I know we felt so thankful that we were amazingly protected and lived to tell about it. What a frightening ordeal!

Trip to the Post Office

One day when I was making a quick visit to the local post office, I got out of my car as usual and headed for the door. Because it was a fairly busy office most of the time, there were several people around, some going in and some coming outside.

I was not paying too much attention, but I noticed a burly, somewhat disheveled man with dark, curly hair standing near the front door. He had on a typical looking trench coat, with what appeared to be a white undershirt peeking through at the top, although I do not remember it being a particularly bad weather or rainy day. He started coming toward me rather quickly, which was when I got a better look at him.

The man appeared rattled, and clutched his coat as he barreled toward me. But just as he came near me as I was about half way to the door from my car, he suddenly stopped fast. He looked right at me, and his face went pale. He gasped and I saw fear in his eyes, as he turned around and hurried off the other way. I do not know what he saw or why he had been coming toward me in such a rush. But I know he saw something which made him stop.

Maybe he was going to grab my purse or my keys to try to steal my car. I was young and may have looked like an easy target. Or maybe he was a flasher and was going to open his coat to shock me. I do not know. Maybe he was not even coming for me. But I know something suddenly stood between the two of us and changed his plan, whether it was something angelic or imagined. I did not see it, but I did see his reaction, and I will never forget the look on his face. Whatever he saw, I was so thankful it was there to help keep me safe that day.

Under the Influence

As I grew into adulthood, I was restless and dissatisfied with life. I had my faith, or at least I thought I had it at the time. But I did not realize how unaware I was, and I was always wanting to achieve more and find what I envisioned as success. I had not yet learned that the journey is what counts, not the destination.

I had gone back to school to earn my degree, but other than that, I did not have a lot of close friends or much of a life. So other than work, I loved to go out for fun and to hear live music. Most of my friends had similar lives, and we spent way too much time drinking together.

I lived only a few miles up the road from a little neighborhood bar. Even if my friends and I would go to other restaurants or venues during an evening, we would usually all end up at this one little place at the end of the night. There was music there on the weekends, and occasionally, if I ever went there on a weekday, the same patrons were always there. So I knew most everyone and it was sort of like being around a family of people.

I do not know how many times I got in my car and drove home after drinking way too much. I cringe when I think about it now. I was so stupid and could have easily killed someone on the road or myself. I lived so close by, yet anything could have happened when I was behind the wheel. It makes me feel sad and embarrassed that I was such an unaware, selfish and pitiful person feeling the need to live that way.

It simply amazes me when I look back at all those times...times when I never got stopped by the police, not one time. I deserved to go to jail, and I do not know if God knew I would be unable to emotionally handle it or if He wanted me to see how only He could keep me safe. Some people call it luck, but I know better.

My Sweet Dog

Wanting to find a career instead of just a job, I applied for a position as a flight attendant with the airlines. When I went to the interview, I was told that if I was hired, I would need to report to work three months later. So I went ahead with it, thinking that I would have time to get my affairs in order, even if it meant relocating.

After a long day of several interviews going through the hierarchy of the process, I went home and pondered my answers to all the questions I had been asked. I wondered if I even stood a chance or if they had realized that I really do not like to fly.

A few days later, on a Thursday, I got the call and was offered a position. I was so excited because it would be more money than I had been making. It would have also offered more excitement in my life and I knew it would give long-term employment and benefits. Then the caller dropped the bomb...she said I needed to report in OREGON the following MONDAY for several weeks of training.

I lived in California by myself at the time, and I had an apartment full of belongings to pack and put into storage. More importantly, I could not abandon my dog, Zinfandel, who was also my best friend. I could not afford to put her in a kennel nor did I want to do that. Even if I could have found a temporary home for her, she was older and would not handle a transition like that well.

It was so upsetting and such a huge disappointment to have to make a choice. To this day, I do not know why they had said one thing and then immediately changed the agenda. I obviously would not have even interviewed if I had known when I might have had to start training. When I asked to go to their next class because there was no way I could get to Oregon so fast, they simply told me that I was welcome to apply again at a later date.

I ended up staying in California and my life went in a completely different direction than I thought it would have had I taken that position. I did not understand it at the time, but God used my sweet dog who I loved so much to help me choose my path, although I had no idea where I was going next. My dog lived several more years after that and brought me great joy.

The Shoe Salesman

In my twenties, I was living by myself in a studio apartment, and one day I got a phone call from a nice sounding man. I did not know him, but he introduced himself and explained that he had a particular line of shoes he was selling. He went on to ask me my preferences and size in shoes and if I had heard of his company before. I had not, so I listened as he told me all about it.

We talked for a long time. He seemed very nice and he had a great sense of humor. I do remember hearing what I thought was a lawn blower on his end of the line, and he said his "office" was right by a window. So I dismissed the noise and did not think any more about it.

We had been on the phone for almost an hour, when he asked if we could meet. He said he had enjoyed our conversation and would like to give me, as a gift, a pair of his shoes to try. Being young and so naïve, I was flattered and thought nothing could possibly be odd about that!

I agreed to meet him at a local restaurant. I at least knew enough to meet in a public place. When I got there, he met me inside the restaurant. He was dressed in a suit and tie, although he had a kind of wild-eyed look about him. But he was as friendly in person as he was on the phone. So we got a table and ordered coffee and began to chat.

He handed me a box and said it was for me. I opened it up and there was a pair of beige shoes in my size. They looked like they had a store company name which I thought I had seen before at Target. But again, being so dumb, I was flattered and surprised that he actually had brought me a present.

We sat talking for a short time, and then he suggested he go put the shoes in my car for me. I thought that seemed like a nice idea. So without hesitation, like a complete idiot, I handed him my keys. Not just my car key either, but all of my keys including my house key and other important ones.

I had no idea who this person was or what his game was at the time. I do not know what he did while in my car or if he was looking for something in particular. Maybe he wanted to see my registration to get an address of where I lived or was going to actually steal my car. But thankfully, a few minutes later, he came back in and sat down after putting the shoes in my car.

When we finished our coffee, he asked if I wanted to go to another restaurant and maybe have a bite to eat. I had been having fun talking, and still did not even think anything was unusual about meeting this new salesman, so I agreed to go. We got outside and he asked if I would mind driving, and said he would leave his car there in the parking lot, although I never did see if he had a car there or not. It seemed fine to me, and we both got in my car and drove away together.

He directed me to a restaurant which was not too far away, saying he really liked the food there. It was a solitary building up a hill, and when we arrived, the restaurant was closed. It looked like there were two or three cars in the parking lot, but we did not see any people. We parked and both got out of the car, as he said I should still see the view even if we could not eat there.

At that point, this stranger could have raped or strangled me and could have left me for dead, and no one would have even known what had happened to me. I had not even left any clues as to where I had gone or who I had gone to meet since I did not know myself. Perhaps he did not hurt me or leave me there alone because people had seen us together at the previous restaurant. I do not know. All I do know is that I put myself in a very dangerous situation, yet, nothing bad happened to me and I lived to tell about it. Maybe he was just a very lonely man, who had a strange way of meeting women.

Fortunately, I never heard from that man again, especially considering he may have copied my house key. But I learned to be more aware and careful, although sadly, it still took me quite a while. That man must have had some agenda to have gone to such lengths to make up such an elaborate story. I still cringe when I think about how stupid I was and all that could have happened. I just know that God was with me and took good care of me that evening, even more than I probably know, and I am so grateful.

A Night at the Club

My life was a series of bad choices, one after the other. I had not set out to be rebellious or irresponsible. I was working regularly but felt incredibly unfulfilled, and the people I spent time with had issues of their own. They were good, fun loving people, but were not too happy at the time either and had their own vices that I knew nothing about.

There was a nightclub where my girlfriends and I would go together. We would spend hours getting ready to go, getting dressed and doing our hair and makeup. I would go without giving it too much thought since I was a part of the group and that was what they all wanted to do. So I would go and drink and dance and pretty much make a fool of myself hoping to be noticed. Unknown to me, my friends would go in the bathroom and take drugs while we were there, which later helped explain why they acted so crazy. But even they thought I was too naïve to include me in that. Looking back, of course, that was a good thing.

I was friendly and took most everything at face value. I had experienced some bad situations but still gave people the benefit of the doubt until they proved me wrong. I had such low self-esteem and thought that life would somehow be different when I found that special someone to make my life complete. To that end, I did not have super high expectations and was always a big fan of the underdog. Of course, I hoped to meet "Prince Charming" who had it all. But at that point, it really did not matter. I just wanted someone to want me. So I would make myself available and not think twice about talking to any guy who approached me.

One particular evening, there was a certain man there at the club on a night I was there with my friends. It was a major wake-up call when we found out the next morning that he had taken a random girl out of the club that night we were there and had brutally murdered her in the parking lot.

My friends and I had gone home the night before at closing time not knowing anything had happened. But the story showed up on the news the next day and I began feeling the recognition of having been around such evil without knowing it. I saw by the pictures that the suspect was a nice looking man, and I know in my heart that if he had approached me and talked nicely, I would have been flattered and would have undoubtedly followed him outside too.

I have always felt that the poor murdered girl could have been me. I do not recall seeing that man that night, maybe because I was drinking, maybe just because he did not come near me. But I know I was acting stupid and trying to draw attention to myself. I had to have appeared pathetic and like an easy mark, so it is a real blessing that I survived the night. Somehow, some way, I was either invisible or unattractive to that killer. Thank God!

Providence

Attempted Rape

In my thirties, I was living in a two-bedroom townhouse with a roommate. It was an old and quiet complex in a decent part of town. I did not know a lot of our neighbors, but I saw a few of them occasionally as I walked in and out to my car in the parking lot. I also often saw one of the maintenance men who worked there. He was a young, Hispanic man in his twenties, was quiet and smiled a lot, but we never really had conversations other than to wave at each other. I don't even know if he spoke English or not.

One day, when my roommate left to go to work, it was only a couple of minutes later when I got a knock on the door. I looked out the peephole and saw the familiar face of the young man, so I opened the door to see what he wanted. I did not see his usual smile and nothing was said, but he grabbed me and pushed me into the room behind me.

He was holding one of my arms tightly and started to grab at my pants. I was fighting him but was trying to talk to him to calm him down and to not escalate the situation further. He started unzipping his own pants and pulled his "weapon" out, clearly with the intent of raping me.

I had no idea what to do, and simply grabbed it in an attempt to keep it where I could see it. It was all happening so fast, but I started acting like I was pleasantly surprised. I said, "Wow, look at you" and "You're really excited." I do not know if he understood me and he looked somewhat confused, maybe because of my tone. But he still had my arm tightly in his grip. As I was holding on to him, he again reached for my pants and pulled them down to my knees.

At that point, I do not know what happened or what he thought as he looked at my underwear, looked back at me, and looked at my underwear again. He mumbled something and I just looked at him, and with a look of confusion he let go of me, pulled away and zipped his pants as he ran to the door.

I am convinced that he saw something that I did not see. Otherwise, there was absolutely no reason for him to stop and run away. I could not explain it (then or now), and although the situation was bad enough, I was so thankful to have been spared the horrible violation that could have followed.

Taking a Hike

Yosemite is one of the most amazing places in the world. People visit from everywhere and it is an experience not to be forgotten. There are gorgeous panoramic views, hiking trails up the mountains and several waterfalls several stories high that feed the river below. You can camp there or stay in more traditional lodging, although reservations well in advance are required for either.

One spring, not long after I had married my (then) husband, we were hiking up to Vernal Falls. It is a huge waterfall that has a trail alongside the moving water all the way up the mountain. The steps to the top are cut into the rock and are wide, but there is only a simple railing between the hiker and the cliff overlooking the falls (at least that was all there was at that time). The spray of the falls often makes the steps wet depending on which way the wind blows.

There were a lot of people hiking up the trail, and when we got to the top of the first part it, we sat down to have a snack. At that point, you can stop to rest and either keep going up the trail to the top of the mountain or you can turn around and go back down. We rested a bit and I started feeling very tired. So we started back down the trail and when we got about half way down the hill, I slipped on the wet step.

Keep in mind, at that time, there was nothing to keep people from falling off the cliff into the waterfall and river below except for a thin railing. There was nothing else to grab on to, and a fall like that would most likely kill even the most experienced athlete, as it has in the past.

I could feel myself slip and start to fall. I do not know what exactly happened, but I fell quickly backwards and landed flat on my back, as if I was pushed and held down. I laid there, stunned, thoughts racing through my mind about what could have just happened.

I believe and felt that a force I could not see had held me there in place, and I will be forever grateful for my life being spared that day. Whenever I go anywhere now, especially hiking, I am much more cautious and thoughtful about each step, and I do not take my safety for granted.

Domestic Violence

I grew up in a dysfunctional family where tension and violence became the norm all too often. Fighting and yelling were just a way of life, and it made me sad and afraid. Even though it was something I hated, I had no idea it was taking such a toll on me.

When I went out on my own and began dating, I naturally thought I would find my "knight in shining armor" and would have the perfect life. But as it often happens, I always gravitated toward men who were completely wrong for me.

Years later, I found out how damaged I had been psychologically, and finally figured out how to break that cycle. But for many, many years, it was one bad experience after another, and I brought it all on myself.

I always would try to find the good aspects of men I dated, regardless of how badly they treated me. I unconsciously was looking for someone like my father, and thought that the dysfunction I encountered was normal. So without realizing it, I kept perpetuating the negativity in my life even when thinking I wanted peace and stability.

When I was married to my now ex-husband, our life together was no different. We would argue all the time, in fact, I even remember arguing on our way to getting married. But the funny thing is, I still got married! That should give you some clue as to my feelings about myself at that time.

We would often argue and then make up. That was our life together. But as the years went by, the arguments would get worse, ending up in knockdown, drag out fights. More than once, I was battered and bruised and had a gun held to my head. It was bad. Even my ex-husband's family told me I needed to leave him.

But I believed he did love me, and I wanted our marriage to work. I still hung on to that warped, idealistic idea that love conquers all, and thought that was what relationships were all about because of watching my parents go through it. So I stayed. My ex would apologize, we would make up and then things would erupt again.

One time, my husband had bought a little boat, and one weekend we went camping up to a nearby lake. We got there and had set up camp, and left the trailer and boat parked while we took a drive around the lake. We began arguing about something, and as usual, it escalated quickly. I do not remember the specifics, but I triggered something and my husband got really mad again.

Even though he was driving through a parking lot, he slammed on the brakes in the middle of an aisle, opened the door, grabbed me by my hair and threw me out of his truck. Then he started to drive off. There just happened to be a park ranger nearby who saw it all happening.

Fortunately, I did not break any bones when I fell. I got pretty scraped up though, and was bleeding when the ranger approached me. That angel who came to my rescue made sure I was all right, even though I was quite shaken. He told me he had called the local police and that they were on their way.

The ranger took me to our camp site, where my husband had gone when he had driven off and left me on the ground. We got there at about the same time as the police, who arrested my husband and took him to jail.

As they drove away, I remember my husband sitting in the back of the police car, handcuffed and yelling obscenities at me. I did not know how long he would be gone or what would happen next, but I knew I did not want to stay at the camp alone. So I packed up everything, including the tent and all our bulky and heavy gear. I had absolutely no idea how to connect the boat trailer to the truck, but I somehow got it hooked up.

I did not know how to pull a trailer, plus I was still so shaky from hurting, crying and hurrying to pack. I was in no shape to drive, but all I wanted to do was get home. It is all a bit of a blur, but I remember driving home on the freeway. I do not remember anyone else helping me get ready to go, but I honestly do not know how I could have done it by myself. It was just another one of those situations where I was clearly given an extra measure of strength to handle what I needed to accomplish.

You would think that experience would have been enough to show me that I needed to walk away from that marriage. Sadly, it took me a lot longer to gain the strength and insight to figure things out. A lot more happened and things got worse before they got better. But I am so thankful that I got through it and can relate to other women dealing with similar issues.

Happy Baby

I was married to a man who was very charming, but who had some serious issues. Sadly, when we got married I did not know that he was addicted to prescription pain killers. It was something which tainted every area of our lives. He also had a good friend in a similar situation, who ended up dying after a bad car crash because he was driving under the influence. Even that did not make my husband want to get help for himself.

It was a very dark time in my life and I felt very helpless. I loved my husband, but he spent money recklessly and put us into debt (of course, on my credit cards). He drove a truck for a living and infidelity became an issue, which he adamantly denied until I had proof. To make matters worse, he had two children at the time from different mothers. So I should have known ours was a marriage doomed from the beginning. But I was naïve enough to think that only love mattered and that I would be a good influence and things would work out.

He was a heavy smoker, which was also something I hated. I realize there are many types of addiction, and smoking is such a filthy, disgusting habit that affects everything around it, let alone what it does to the body. Often times, this man would take a handful of pills and conk out on the couch with a lit cigarette in his hand. I was so worried that he would burn our home down and kill himself or us both.

He was able to pick up his baby boy every other weekend or so. I was always happy to see such an adorable child, although those were stressful times since it was never clear if my husband was going to be responsible and care for him appropriately. The baby was less than a year old at the time and needed constant attention. My husband would play with him, but always with a cigarette in hand. Even though he needed to care for his little baby boy, he still would take a handful of pills and conk out, leaving the baby unsupervised and completely vulnerable.

I cannot count how many times I would come home from work to find my husband out cold on the couch and the baby just crawling around on the floor or sitting crying in a corner. It was so heartbreaking and it scared me to death. Not only could my husband have caused a fire, but the baby could have wandered away or hurt himself and my husband would not even have known until it was too late.

With everything going on, the frustrations became unbearable and were met with violence toward me. It was shocking since I could not believe my life began to closely resemble what I had seen my own mother go through. It was such a low period and was the only time that suicide ever remotely crossed my mind. Anyone who knows me knows that my faith in God is strong and I truly believe suicide never solves anything and is never an option.

Although the marriage was not my happiest or proudest decision in life, I relied on my faith and finally chose divorce as the solution in order to keep my sanity. I finally learned that a sick person has to want to get well, and no matter how badly you might want it for them, they must take responsibility and take the necessary action. Otherwise, it will never happen.

For whatever reason, the mother of this child who I cared for during our four year marriage must have been quite jealous of me. We were always cordial with each other, but when my husband and I got divorced, she did not want me to see her child ever again. I was crushed because I had loved him like he was my own. I do not think his mother ever realized how at risk he had often been while in my husband's care or else she just did not appreciate my participation in his life.

It still makes me sad to this day, although I have tried to understand her point of view. I hope my one-time stepson is as happy an adult as he was as a baby, and I am glad he was in my life to give me joy and perspective when I needed it.

Learning the Hard Way

I went through an ordeal which left me involved in a court case. But we did come to an agreement, and part of the settlement was confidentiality. So unfortunately, I cannot publish my story about it. But I can write about some tips I have learned through the years.

Like many people, I have been swindled by more con-artists than I like to admit. Part of that has been because I was so naive, and partly just because I was simply too trusting. Even when asking friends for referrals, I sometimes still found myself dealing with dishonest people who ultimately took advantage of me.

I have had bad experiences with doctors, attorneys, maintenance people, call center reps, bankers, musicians, salesmen, even police officers...you name it. If they were out there, I somehow found them (or they found me). Naturally, they each presented themselves as professional when I first met them. But in the end, they did not deliver on their promises.

Unfortunately, there really is no absolute when it comes to finding good people. Obviously, you should ask friends for referrals and hope they can steer you in a good

direction.   But   even   referrals   might   deal
differently with you than they have with others,
depending on their current circumstances.

Most business people leave clues behind as
well. So it is worth it to take the time to do your
due diligence and ask around and to even ask
for references from them and the places where
they have previously worked. But be alert, since
they may have you call someone you think is a
business reference and in reality is just their
"couch potato brother" covering for them. But
it still is a good idea to at least ask.

Of   course,   you   want   someone   who   is
professional,   sober,   honest,   reliable,
trustworthy, sharp and positive, regardless of
the profession. If a business person has been
around for any length of time, they will have at
least begun to establish their reputation within
the community. You should also be able to
check with the local Chamber of Commerce,
Better Business Bureau or similar professional
organization to inquire about them and ask if
they are aware of any complaints regarding
that business or person.

You really have to be aware and trust your
instincts. Often when someone begins a job,
things will be fine. But as they go along, you
may begin to have questions or start to see
small deficiencies. Never be afraid to ask

questions, and a job may need to be stopped before it is really begun or finished, regardless of how inconvenient. The time and/or cost you may incur may be cheaper in the long run, than having them finish the job only to find out it has to be fixed or redone anyway.

The bottom line is that you have to value yourself and know who you are in dealing with people and set your expectations, no matter what arena you are in. You do not want to compromise your needs because someone else has no integrity. There are a lot of unscrupulous people out there, and you simply cannot be too careful. Especially in the digital and social era we are living in, often times, people misrepresent themselves.

Just because someone wears the right clothes and looks a certain way or calls himself a professional, does not mean they are one. Feel free to get a second opinion. The good news is that there are also still so many good people in the world, but you should never apologize for asking questions and protecting yourself. Even when it feels uncomfortable or unnecessary, it is better to be safe than sorry later on.

Providence

My Path to Positivity

Looking back, we can always see more clearly how things in our lives work together. I never realized it until recently, but along with so many experiences and influences, I was being prepared for my passions of today.

Once I discovered personal development and really understood the positive psychology movement, I quickly became aware of how transformation can take place in a person's life. I still study with mentors to deepen my knowledge and practice every day.

But because I had such a tumultuous life growing up, it took me a very long time to learn to think for myself. It wasn't until much later that I learned how to change my thinking and behavior and become victorious over my circumstances.

At one point while I was still living at home, my mother started going to church at Garden Grove Community Church, later known as the Crystal Cathedral. The Reverend Robert H. Schuller was the lead pastor of that church, so we got the benefit of hearing his uplifting sermons most every week. He often spoke of his own mentor and the teachings of Dr. Norman Vincent Peale.

The church had an amazing music department, and they often had special celebrity guests to perform on their programs which were broadcast across the globe. People who went to church there, either in person or by television, got to hear the message of hope, inspiration and the love of Jesus Christ.

Countless times in my many years at that church, I was inspired and motivated, not only by Dr. Schuller, but by the beautiful musical performances I got to enjoy. Looking back, I see now how important Dr. Schuller was in my development, and may have been one of the few people who helped me get through my many challenges.

Years later, I have studied positive psychology and personal growth in depth with many mentors. I have seen such dramatic results in my own life and am so excited to now share it with others. I realize that most people merely exist and really never learn how to transform and truly live their own lives. But real change is possible when we allow the Spirit to work within us.

God truly uses every experience in our lives and nothing is wasted. All those years, I never thought a thing about teaching what I was learning, but now I see how God was using my time with Dr. Schuller and his ministry to really prepare me for my future.

Providence

Unconditional Love

I was blessed with the best grandparents on earth. They were my mother's parents, and they were incredibly fine people. They brought my mother up well as an only child and were extremely influential in my life.

I remember my father's parents as well, although they were divorced and both lived in different areas of the country. So we only saw them occasionally and were not able to spend as much time together.

From as far back as I can remember, my maternal grandparents were present in my life. They were babysitters for my brother and me when we were young while my parents worked, and we would all often sit around the dinner table as a family on Sunday afternoons.

My grandfather was a salesman and occasionally took us to his office. My grandmother was a wonderful homemaker and cook, who loved to care for her family. I have sweet memories of being at their home, playing croquet out on the lawn, playing with toy trains and smelling my grandmother's gorgeous roses in their garden. Many of the simple joys I treasure today are similar to what I shared with my grandparents.

It took me years to understand why these two adorable people would always celebrate their anniversary on my grandmother's birthday. I realized much later in life that they had eloped when my Grandma had turned eighteen years old. Her family had not been happy that she was seeing an older fellow. But they began to accept him when they suddenly had a new son-in-law and they quickly grew to love him.

My grandparents were strong Christians and shining role models of their faith. They were loving and helpful, yet strict and unwavering. A lot of why I grew up with strong values and beliefs myself was due to their consistent example despite my parents' volatile relationship.

When I was older and began questioning those beliefs, I could be pretty obstinate and rebellious. But I actually stayed out of trouble sometimes because the thought of disappointing my grandparents was always in the back of my mind. I could hear them reminding me that God knows our hearts and sees everything, and that we are to be good stewards of all we have been given.

During some of the worst times in my life, I could always count on my grandparents to love and support me unconditionally. They were such positive role models for me. As much as anyone, I was crushed when they went home to be with the Lord. But I have great joy remembering them and knowing that we will be reunited one day soon.

I am so grateful that God used these incredibly loving and humble people to guide and teach me so much. I can only hope to be remotely like them and have a just a fraction of their impact in the world.

Providence

Another Musician

Having worked at Disneyland for a very long time should have given me stability. But I always had such a restless spirit and thought I should be making more of myself. At the time, as people often do, I imagined that the answer was simply about making more money.

I got a part-time job at a restaurant as a cocktail server, hoping to make a lot in tips. But I learned quickly that I had to split any I made with other workers. There was live music there on the weekends, which brought in business and made the job a lot more fun. I got to know some of the musicians a little bit if they returned to play more than one night.

I only worked at that restaurant for a short while. But one of the bands was there a few times and I got to know them since two of the members were women. I enjoyed their music and they made me laugh, and I invited my friends to also come hear them while I worked. But then after I fell and was injured, I left that job.

A couple years went by, and a friend called one day to ask if I wanted to go with her to hear that same band play. She remembered them and had seen an ad saying they would be at a local hangout the following weekend. So we made plans to go.

When we arrived, we noticed that there was one new band member. He was a tall, lean, singing machine who played the bass guitar. It turned out that he did not work with that band too much longer. But I did get to know him over a period of time and we discovered we had a thirty year history in common even though we had just met. To make a long story short, he is now my husband!

That was one of those situations where there is no way you can see how the pieces fit together until you are able to look back at them. It was almost as if I was working at the restaurant just to meet the people in that band, and my husband was only with them a short time to meet me. Somehow it all worked out and came together. Coincidence? I think not! However it happened, I am so thankful to have a wonderful life partner who is very dear and good for me.

A Special Hug

As a Christian, I believe that the Bible is a living document, and is the true, current and relevant Word of God. The Holy Spirit speaks to Believers individually through various passages, addressing specific needs.

One such time for me was several years back when I was traveling alone to Texas for a job training. I was very nervous about what to expect, so my fear of flying didn't help much. But I was excited about my new work position and anxious to get where I was going.

The flight was very early in the morning, and I got to the airport with time to spare, which is pretty unusual for me. As I sat on the plane getting ready for take-off, I was praying and starting to read my Bible while other passengers were still boarding.

I felt a strong direction in my mind to turn to Psalm 139. As I began reading the Scripture, verses 9-10 jumped out at me. They talk about "taking the wings of the morning" and how God's "right hand shall hold me."

Some skeptics would say that I was just seeing what I wanted to see in that moment. But my eyes welled up with tears and I felt an overwhelming sense of peace as I knew I was not alone. I could relax and dwell on those sweet words of comfort and enjoy the flight.

I have similar experiences all the time and Christianity is a very personal faith. It is not about a religion, but is a relationship with the living God. Other words from that particular chapter talk about "how precious" are God's thoughts toward us, and I felt it so closely that day on the plane like a big hug. That Psalm is one of my favorites and I read it often because it is so special to me. I remember those words whenever I start to feel lonely or discouraged.

Discovering Me

I had joined a network marketing and sales company and had high hopes of becoming a huge success there. Little did I know that I would become successful, just not in the way I had expected. One of the best parts of the direct sales industry is that a big part of it includes personal development training. The more you learn about and work on your own personal growth, the better your life and career can become. It seems like such a simple concept, but most people miss it entirely or simply give up on it.

I had always enjoyed learning but was not aware that personal development was something different than mere academics. I had graduated from college and taken classes toward an advanced degree. I liked to read but always felt I was too busy, and actually was included in the statistics which say that most people never read another book after getting out of school. I had to learn to develop my mind and that success is so much more than society's labels.

My mentors were successful people, both financially and in life, so I was anxious to learn from them. They explained that personal development is not a difficult process. But it does require a commitment to yourself and to planning and taking the time required to see growth happen.

Every bit of information you think about matters, so you should concentrate on the books you read, the information you watch and hear and the people with whom you associate. All of these things have a profound impact on you, and you have to become skilled at what you allow into your mind. It is a process, and growth occurs over time. But the key to all of it is consistency. That really is the hardest part and what people struggle with the most. But it does pay off if you stick with it.

Once you begin to see progress, personal development really becomes exciting and somewhat addicting. You realize that a different way of thinking and living truly is possible, and it makes you want to continue your journey even more. Now I personally look forward to my reading every single day, and I feel deprived when I do not get it done. I have read many good books during the past few years and my associations and mentors today continue to make me a better person.

Personal development is truly life changing, and it has brought out the real me who had been buried deep inside for so long. I am a completely different person now than who I was for most of my life. I realize the possibilities available to me and I love living. I look forward to the future and am so thankful I learned about personal growth and can share the power of it with others.

Providence

The Slamming Door

When my husband and I first moved to the southern California desert, we began attending a large church in the area and went there for several years. We loved it. But sadly, as it often happens, things began to change when a series of new pastors were brought in. We felt sad and disappointed about that and felt led to change churches.

We were excited when a brand new church was starting right up the street from us. Because it was so close and convenient, we thought God had answered our prayers asking for direction about where to go next. We found that the lead pastor there was an amazing speaker and was very inspiring. We really got a lot out of his sermons.

We not only began to regularly attend services there, but we also went to the new member class to find out about joining the church. We wanted to volunteer, so we went to additional classes offered to see where we might fit in to serve.

But for weeks, we never heard from anyone at the church. We would ask about it all on Sundays when we saw the different pastors and they would always make excuses, saying it was something simply overlooked or they would refer us to someone in the office. So we would wait, but still, no one would return our calls or communicate with us.

Because my husband is a musician, he had hoped to be a part of the worship team as he had been at our previous church. But there was never any communication or follow through in that department either. The whole time, we prayed for God to direct us where He wanted us to go, and that if we should not be at that church, to make it clear.

After months of trying to be a part of that congregation, it was becoming quite obvious that we were not meant to attend there. It seemed so odd, but everything seemed so disorganized and it was as if we were invisible to those people. So we continued to pray for direction but could not help but wonder why the situation was not working out.

One day, out of the blue, we got a call from a pastor we had known from our previous church who had been our worship pastor. He asked if my husband was currently playing anywhere and if he could come play with the musicians at his new church. So we went to visit there and found it to be a perfect fit for us. We have attended and served there now for several years.

When you listen to and watch for what God is showing you, often signs are very subtle. But then again, sometimes they are a little more dramatic so there can be no question about the answer. Sometimes the door has to slam shut for another one to open. We are very happy at our current church, love serving there and have made a lot of new friends. We are so thankful God led us there.

Providence

Just Like Moses

When I got married again, both my husband and I worked from home, so we could pretty much live anywhere. At the time when we moved to the desert, we had looked at new homes in several areas. We had gone to northern California, Arizona, Nevada and had looked locally in southern California.

Most new homes being built at that time were huge, two-story floor plans. We wanted a one-story plan which was not quite so large. So when we finally walked into the model of our future home, we knew right away it was the house for us. We were excited to move to a new area, even though it took sixteen months for our house to be finished.

We visited the site several times during the building process. We took pictures of everything and even realized when the builders made mistakes so we could have issues fixed right away. During those many months, we experienced the extremes in the weather which happen in the desert, although we still looked forward to moving there.

I soon realized that we were far away from life as I knew it. It was not that far a distance in miles or in time away. But it was far enough to find out who were my real friends. I stayed in contact with a few people, but for the most part, I soon lost touch and realized I was starting over. Even to this day, some family members and friends still have never visited our home and rarely even correspond with us.

My husband and I made a new life for ourselves and got to know new neighbors, people at church and in the community. I had never had a lot of close friends anyway, but missed the people I thought of as special people in my life. I had not realized how most things I had done previously were in an effort to make other people happy and what an influence those friends had been. I had never learned to put my own needs first, and like most people, I must have thought that success would simply happen to me if I worked hard enough.

As a couple, we were busy in our new life with work and had fortunately learned about personal development. It became routine to read and study together and to strive for growth. In fact, we still work to continue it together every day. I sometimes felt lonely without my friends, but because it was just the two of us, it forced me to examine my own life and learn who I was, what I wanted and my purpose for being. Looking back, I realize some of those people I missed so much never really were my friends at all, and now I know how to tell the difference.

My faith was always strong. But it was not until I had been brought out to the desert and forced to look within myself that I began to finally understand true success. I learned what it meant to really have a daily walk with God and consequently, He has changed my perspective on many things since then.

If you are familiar with the Bible, it did not take me quite as long as it took Moses when he was in the desert, but I am so grateful that God was so patient and faithful in my life through my own journey and past mistakes. He continues to be with me now, and I strive to give Him glory for the person He is making of me and for all He has done in my life.

Providence

You Never Know

My husband and I held meetings for our company when we were active in direct sales. They were always a big part of our business, even though they were a lot of work. No one else in the area would do that job, even people with more experience than we had. But we needed a weekly meeting and stepped up to handle that responsibility for our area. Those meetings went on for several years.

We would often have speakers come out for support from other cities and we enjoyed the time we got to spend with them. Most of the people who joined us were successful in the business, so it was always a learning experience as well.

There were certain regulars from our local area who would attend the meetings. It became a family of sorts, and we all had fun together as well as hoping to increase business in the region. Several of us would go out to eat after the meetings. There was one particular young woman who came occasionally. She was pretty and seemed demure and the men often vied for her attention.

We saw a lot of the same people at company national conventions once or twice a year. One time, that certain young lady was there and we were with her when she met a handsome leader in the business who was about her same age. They seemed to hit it off right away, and we could see the look of enchantment in their eyes toward each other.

The two started dating, and whenever we saw them together, she would watch her new interest like a hawk. She soon began to seem obsessed and very possessive of him, although still never saying much directly to us. After a while, much to her dismay, the young man tried to distance himself and break off the relationship with her.

She then started showing up at our local meetings again, but with several other men who came out to speak for us. It seemed very odd and her demeanor was different and more flirtatious than before, as if she wanted to make her previous flame jealous. Rarely, did he even come to our meetings because he lived far away. But since it was such a tight knit group of people, she must have thought word would somehow get back to him.

One time my husband and I had planned to meet the scheduled speaker for dinner before our meeting, and when we arrived, this same woman had come with him. We were surprised, but we talked and laughed and had a good time. It did not seem to even cross her mind that we might be wondering about her various relationships. Her personal life was really none of our business, so we did not ask questions.

But soon after that, we went to a training and sadly heard the news that the young man she had been seeing originally had been brutally murdered. Sadly, this young, beautiful girl, who had her entire life ahead of her, was the first person everyone thought of who knew the situation. It took a while for the police to put all the evidence together and even longer to get the case to trial, but this woman has since been arrested and convicted of first degree murder and will spend the rest of her life in prison.

It is still so hard to believe that we could repeatedly be duped and in the presence of someone capable of such dangerous and destructive behavior. It is just as frightening that we could spend close time together in fellowship and actually enjoy ourselves unwittingly. Even though we were not the intended targets, we were so thankful to have been unharmed, because we know this type of tragedy could have included any number of people along the way.

It is a horrific reminder that until you know someone really well (and even when you do), you have to be alert and cautious because you really never know what a person is capable of doing. We count ourselves fortunate, but hold our murdered friend's family in thought and prayer, as we will never forget such a good man who was manipulated and destroyed.

Tire Trouble

One day while I was driving in town, the tire light came on in my car. I was not too alarmed since it sometimes lights up simply due to slight climate changes. But since I was alone that day, I hoped the light did not mean I had a flat tire.

As I kept driving, I did not feel any difference in the ride or hear any noises coming from my car. I felt that was a good sign. But I thought I would pull over to the side of the road and visually check to see if there was any damage.

I pulled into the next driveway and parked my car. I got out and walked around the vehicle to see if any of my tires were low, but they all appeared fine. I then promptly called my husband to let him know what was happening, and to say I would call him back if I had any trouble as I continued driving.

The tire light stayed on, and I started driving toward home which was still several miles away. I was going the speed limit, but was starting to feel a little nervous and was wishing I could get there more quickly. I proceeded cautiously, still listening for any unusual noises from under the car, but there were none.

It seemed like it took a lot longer than usual to get home. But I finally got to our neighborhood gate without any problems, and just as I entered our street, I began hearing a thumping sound. I continued driving up the street toward our house, and the noise got louder and louder and I started to feel an unevenness in the ride.

Because I was so close to home by that time, I wanted to try to keep going in hopes that I might make it all the way there. I got to where I was only three houses away from home, when the noise was so loud and the thump felt so strong that I knew I had to stop or ruin my tire rim.

When I got out of the car to see what the tire looked like, I saw that it was completely shredded. Whatever it was that had gotten into my tire had happened at least several miles before, but God had brought me home, literally, so I was safe and sound and not stuck on the side of the road by myself someplace in the dark. What a blessing! I was able to call my husband who was there at home waiting, and he was able to walk out to meet me and give me a hug.

Life Today

Always doing my best was just how I functioned, or so I thought. But my personality had been so stunted by living in a dysfunctional home and by being abandoned by my father, and I did not even know it. My own needs were not a priority and I put everybody else in my life first. I always looked to others to be the solutions to any of my problems instead of learning self-love or self-reliance. Consequently, I had no confidence and very low self-esteem.

It took a lot of time and many experiences to help me begin to mature. I had been so sheltered, and even when I got a degree in psychology, I had not truly understood why I had not gotten many good results in life or why I had made a lot of the choices I had made. I had always worked hard and searched for something to make me successful, when I really already had everything I needed. I just had to develop awareness and find what was within myself. Once I discovered personal development, I finally began to understand how to do that, and I learned how to stop reacting to my environment.

I have learned to think differently and I practice that every day. I am open to possibility and opportunity. I have grown to really love myself and appreciate my time alone, as well as with others. I understand people so much better since I learned about myself, and I look forward to learning something new every day.

I enjoy my life now, and I am extremely thankful for my husband, our health, our family, our home, our pets, and all our blessings seen and unseen. I try hard not to take a single thing for granted. I keep very busy and enjoy writing, music, photography, social media and travel, as well as being a homemaker. I also believe in serving and giving back. I volunteer at our church, as a Big Sister with Big Brothers Big Sisters of the Desert, as a Community Ambassador with American Red Cross, with our local Chamber of Commerce and with some of my mentors at their events. So I am blessed with a full life.

I am learning every day how to deal with the aging process, which is often frustrating. But I am also continually learning more and more about how to follow and trust Christ. Although this life is not perfect and I still have many shortcomings, I hope to be an example of God's grace and a testimony of His direction and protection. I feel so fortunate that He has kept

His hand on me all these years, and I look forward to where He will lead me next.

Providence

Epilogue

I cannot exactly remember when I first accepted Jesus into my heart. All I know is that it was the best decision I have or will ever make in my life. I was baptized when I was twelve years old, and took that opportunity to dedicate my life to Christ publicly.

I always had faith and felt God was important to me. I had always known about "walking" with God, which I thought I had done since He was always on my mind and in my heart. But it took me many years to develop a daily, personal relationship with Him, which I finally realized was, and is, the purpose for my life regardless of anything else. I trust Him to continue to lead me and help me use the gifts He has given me. He has been so faithful and has been beside me through everything, and I am so grateful for His love and care. I truly do not know how I would have survived on my own, and these stories testify to that.

If you are struggling or want more in life, hope is available. That is what I know for sure after experiencing so much. My stories give accounts of circumstances which often have no explanation, and what most people call mere coincidence. But they prove to me that I was never alone. I had no idea of my own worth, but clearly, God has always cared and has had a plan for me from the very beginning.

No matter what you are facing, you have to want help and be responsible enough to reach out for it. You may make better decisions than I did growing up, but it is so important to your future to assess where you are right now, where you are going and to trust God to help you make it happen.

There are so many resources available to help you find your way. But the work has to begin, especially if you are in a situation which affects other people as well as yourself. Loneliness, addiction and abuse is rampant and can be devastating. You have to raise your own awareness and when you understand yourself and your true value, the world of opportunity can open up and you can truly live your dreams. Every day matters toward that effort.

The major part of that puzzle is that no matter what choices you have made, God loves you and has designed you with a specific purpose. No one else can do what you were made to do, so you have to be willing to do the work to find out what that purpose is. Then you can become the person you were designed to be, and you will also be surprised when you look back at your amazing journey.

I am so thankful that I was given the opportunity to know and receive Jesus, and that He has preserved my life and allowed me to tell and use my story to help others. I now strive to live for Him and share His message of love. I do not know what the future holds, but I do know that Jesus holds the future. I hope you can know Him too.

Providence

About the Author

Ann Haerr has an extensive background in customer service, and she loves working with people. She discovered her appreciation for excellence early in life while working for Disney, and currently works independently as an author and as an encouragement and transformational coach.

She loves helping people know themselves better and to encourage their self-esteem and confidence in order to help them create lasting change and lead more fulfilling lives. This can make such a difference for anyone in any industry, but is especially important for women who have been neglected or abused who need help understanding how to move forward in life.

Ann is very active in her community and believes strongly in service to others. She considers herself to be a perpetual student and loves to learn. She holds several certifications and received her BA in Psychology from California State University Dominguez Hills, with postgraduate studies in Counseling Psychology from California State University Fullerton. She lives in sunny southern California with her husband and dogs.

Ann is always happy to share her story, and is available for coaching via phone or through Skype. More information can be found on her website, or through various social media platforms. Join her mailing list to be notified of forthcoming projects, events and her new book series, Lazy is Crazy™.

Connect at:

AnnHaerr.com

Facebook.com/AnnHaerrCPC
LinkedIn.com/in/AnnHaerr

Email: AnnHaerr@gmail.com

Providence